Hathaway

W9-DBD-284

A Mediaeval Garden of Herbs from Brunschwig's LIBER DE ARTE DISTILLANDI, Strassburg, Grüninger, 1500

Herbs

FOR THE MEDIAEVAL HOUSEHOLD

FOR COOKING, HEALING
AND DIVERS USES

BY MARGARET B. FREEMAN

THE METROPOLITAN MUSEUM OF ART
NEW YORK

Copyright 1943 by The Metropolitan Museum of Art

Copyright © renewed 1971 by The Metropolitan Museum of Art

Seventh Printing 1979

International Standard Book Number 0-87099-067-5

Acknowledgment

I should like to express my grateful thanks to Mr. E. J. Alexander of the New York Botanical Garden for checking the list of herbs; to Mr. Lathrop Harper for allowing me to study his fine collection of mediaeval herbals; to the staffs of the Pierpont Morgan Library and the Library of the New York Academy of Medicine for their generous assistance; and to my colleague Mrs. Hildegard Schneider, Gardener at The Cloisters, for help beyond the call of duty.

A Discourse on the Virtues of the Rose from Champier's ROSA GALLICA, Paris, Jodocus Badius, 1514

The single herbs illustrated in this book are for the most part from the HORTUS SANITATIS or GART DER GESUNDHEIT published by Peter Schoeffer at Mainz in 1485 (see Introduction). The woodcuts of Sweet Bay, Rue, Savory, Celandine, Stavesacre, and Sweet Woodruff are from the HORTUS SANITATIS printed at Lübeck by Steffen Arndes in 1492. Coriander, Hyssop, and Spurge are from the HERBARIUS published in Mainz by Peter Schoeffer in 1484. From Crescentius's IN COMMODŪ RURALIUM [Speyer, Peter Drach, 1490-1495] are Elecampane, Saffron Crocus, Agrimony, and Cuckoo-Pint. The mediaeval gardeners shown in the Introduction on pages x-xii are also from the edition of Crescentius mentioned above.

"*A Bathe Medicinable*" from REGIMEN SANITATIS, Strassburg, Mathias Hupfuff, 1513

Gathering Herbs from the title-page of the GRETE HERBALL, London, Peter Treveris, 1526

Introduction

"What is an herb?" the scholar Alcuin is said to have inquired of his pupil Charlemagne. The reply was "The friend of physicians and the praise of cooks." This conversation may be apocryphal and not very profound and perhaps even a little ungrammatical but nevertheless Charlemagne's definition of mediaeval herbs is as succinctly true as any that can be found in the herb books today. Charlemagne must have known quite a lot about herbs—or at least one of his advisers did—for he included among his instructions to the royal stewards a list of seventy-four herbs which were to be planted in the imperial gardens. The list has survived as a part of the CAPITULARE DE VILLIS and has been widely published in recent times. This is only a list, however, with no indication of the uses to which the various herbs were put. One must turn to the cookbooks and housebooks and herbals to discover what the mediaeval housewife did with hyssop and fennel and feverfew, with roses and rosemary and rue. ℭ The FORME OF CURY [Cookery], edited by S[amuel] Pegge and printed in London in 1780, is a good example of the mediaeval cookbook. Compiled by the chief master cooks of King Richard II of England in 1390, it explains how to prepare spinach and cabbage as well as the more royal delicacies such as roasted peacock, apple-blossom fritters, and hippocras wine. Among the innumerable recipes which call for herbs, "Douce Ame" is a fair

sample. "Take good cow milk and do it in a pot. Take parsley, sage, hyssop, savoury, and other good herbs and hew them and do them in the milk and seethe them. Take capons half roasted and smite them in pieces and do thereto pyn and honey clarified. Salt it and color it with saffron and serve it forth." For a "salat" take "parsley, sage, garlic, chibolls [small onions], onions, leek, borage, mint, porrette [greens], fennel and cresses, rue, rosemary, purslane. Lave and wash them clean, pick them, pluck them small with thine hand and mingle them well with raw oil, lay on vinegar and salt and serve it forth." The foreword of this cookbook states that it was written with "the assent and advisement of the masters of physic and philosophy that dwell in the King's Court." The colophon asserts: *Explicit coquina que est optima medicina* [Here concludes the art of cookery which is the best medicine]. ⟪Although cookbooks may claim that a good cousine is the best insurance for health, it was to the herbals that the housewife turned for advice on what to do for "feet gouts" and "itching in the seat," for "botches on the face" and "dimness of the eyes," for "drunkenness" and "yexing" and "wicked unchaste dreams." Of the herbals quoted in the following pages, that by the Greek author Dioscorides is the earliest, having been written in the first century A.D. This work includes about five hundred medicinal plants and was accepted as an almost infallible authority throughout the entire Middle Ages. The edition used here is that "englished by John Goodyear A.D. 1655" and edited by Robert T. Gunther, Oxford, 1934. Sometime before the sixth century A.D. an unknown writer usually called Pseudo-Apuleius, who regarded physicians with complete distrust, set down "a few powers of plants and some cures of the body" for his compatriots, so that if any bodily vexation should befall them they might be cured by his science "in spite of the doctors." This herbal was translated into Anglo-Saxon in the eleventh century and rendered into modern English by T. O. Cockayne in LEECHDOMS WORTCUNNING AND STAR-CRAFT OF EARLY ENGLAND, 1864. Its popularity is shown by the number of manuscripts and printed editions produced in the Middle Ages. ⟪Two English herbals valuable for the study of mediaeval herb lore are the GRETE HERBALL, printed by Peter Treveris in 1526, and BANCKES'S HERBAL, printed by Richard Banckes, London [1525]. A modern edition of the latter, edited by Sanford V. Larkey, M.D., and Thomas Pyles, was published by the New

York Botanical Garden in 1941 under the title AN HERBAL [1525]. These herbals describe "how man may be holpen with green herbes of the garden and weeds of the fields as well as by costly receipts of the apothecaries prepared." In their flavorful, lusty, mediaeval English, they give home remedies for everything from "wicked winds of the womb [stomach]" to "wagging teeth." They explain "how to stain or dye your hair or nails a red color" and what to do for "freckles of the visage," "superfluity of flesh," and "falling hair." They are concerned also with making "a man merry," achieving "a good mind," and preserving youth. Their usefulness in the household is apparent. ☾ Many of the quotations and a large proportion of the woodcuts in the following pages are taken from the well-known herbal HORTUS SANITATIS, or GART DER GESUNDHEIT, published by Peter Schoeffer at Mainz in 1485. "Since man can have no greater nor nobler treasure on earth than bodily health," writes the author of this German *Garden of Health,* "I came to the conclusion that I could not perform any more honorable, useful or holy work...than to compile a book in which should be contained the virtue and nature of many herbs ...together with their true color and form, for the help of all the world and the common good." For this worthy project, he employed "a master learned in physic" and "a painter ready of wit, cunning and subtle of hand." (Translation from Agnes Arber, *Herbals.*) Whether or not he succeeded in presenting all the herbs in "their true color and form" according to modern scientific standards, he at least produced the finest set of herbal woodcuts made in the Middle Ages. They were copied and recopied, weaker editions of the originals turning up in herbal after herbal for the next fifty years. ☾ So much for the cookbooks and the herbals. A type of handbook in fashion during the four-

teenth and fifteenth centuries might be called a "Housebook" or "What the Young Bride Should Know about Managing a Home." Such a book is LE MENAGIER DE PARIS, translated by Eileen Power as THE GOODMAN OF PARIS, London, 1928. Written about 1393 by a wealthy, rather elderly bourgeois Parisian for his girl wife, it gives advice on innumerable household problems such as how to plan a dinner party and how to remove spots from clothes, how to take redness out of white wine and caterpillars out of cabbages. Herbs play an important part in this delightful and illuminating volume. The goodman tells the proper time of year for sowing hyssop, fennel, savory, and other herbs. He explains how to grow

rosemary plants from cuttings and how to "keep violets and marjoram in winter against the cold." Most of his menus call for herbs, and his sweet washing-water is made of chamomile or marjoram, rosemary, bay leaves, or sage. Aconite killed his rats and black hellebore his wolves and foxes. Sage cured his toothaches and dried rose petals put in chests perfumed his clothes. There is

much to be learned from the Goodman of Paris. ☾ In Petrus Crescentius's OPUS RURALIUM COMMODORUM, a thirteenth-century treatise on farming and gardening, there is a long section devoted to herbs, "treated according to their existing uses to the human body," and then later, "according to the pleasures they afford to the mind, consequently preserving the health of the body as the state of the body affects the mind." Even in his pleasure garden, Crescentius would plant "a great diversity of medicinal and aromatic herbs which not only please by the odor of their scents, but by their variety of flowers refresh the sight." Among these, "rue should be mingled in many places for its beauty and greenness,

and its bitterness will drive away poisonous animals from the garden." This important work, written by an Italian in Latin, was translated into almost every European language except English and was one of the first books to be printed. The quotations in the following pages are from the Museum's copy in German of the Basel edition of 1512. ☾ From John Russell's BOKE OF NURTURE one finds out about herbal baths. To give your sovereign a "bathe or stewe so-called," says Russell, you should have ready "a basin full in your hand of herbs hot and fresh and with a soft sponge in hand his body...wash." For a "bathe medicinable" one needs hollyhock and mallow, fennel, plantain, chamomile, ground ivy, smallage, wildflax, and a dozen other herbs. "Cast them hot into a vessel," says the author, "and set your sovereign aloft." ☾ Romantic

tales and sober chronicles, love lyrics and drinking songs, also make casual and charming mention of mediaeval uses for herbs. Says a lover to his mistress in a tenth-century song:

"Come, sweetheart, come,
Dear as my heart to me,
Come to the room
I have made fine for thee.
Here there be couches spread,
    Tapestry tented,
Flowers for thee to tread,
Green herbs, sweet scented."

(From Helen Waddell, *Mediaeval Latin Lyrics*). ❧ In Chrétien de Troyes's EREC AND ENIDE "the streets were spread with rushes, mint, and lilies, and curtained with diaper and samite;...never was greater joy." In Boccaccio's DECAMERON "the tables were laid and the whole house strewn with scented plants and exquisite flowers." Malory describes how Queen Guinevere and her knights went a-maying, bedecked "with herbs, mosses and flowers in the best man-

ner and freshest." Chaucer tells of centaury and hellebore and "herb ivy, growing in our yard, that merry is." ❧ From such mediaeval sources as the above, this little book, HERBS FOR THE MEDIAEVAL HOUSEHOLD, has been compiled. It makes no claim to completeness, for that would necessitate a volume of encyclopaedic size. Neither does it pretend to infallibility. Should any reader find that a bath of bay leaves does not cure the colic or rosemary keep away moths, if southernwood fails to "restore where any man lacketh hair" and vervain "to make folk merry at the table," please be indulgent with the mediaeval authors and with me. A certain herbalist says of the "Notions and observations" contained in his work, "most of [these] I am confident are true, and if there be any that are not so, yet they are pleasant."

Gardening and Making Chaplets from Strabo's HORTULUS, Nuremberg, Weyssenburger, 1512

𝕳erbs · xiii

Herbs for Cooking

MANY OF THESE HAVE HEALING VIRTUES ALSO

Mediaeval Cooks from KÜCHENMEISTEREY, Augsburg, Johann
Froschauer, 1507

Anise   Pimpinella Anisum, L.

Anise seed was a highly prized and rather expensive flavoring for food in the Middle Ages. In *The Goodman of Paris* it is sprinkled on meat jellies along with bay leaves and cinnamon; it also appears in a complicated recipe for preserves of nuts, honey, and raisins, with fennel, coriander, and caraway. "The virtue of this herb is thus," states *Banckes's Herbal*, "it unbindeth the stopping of the liver and of wicked winds and of great humours." ℂ Anise is used today in liqueurs such as anisette and ab-

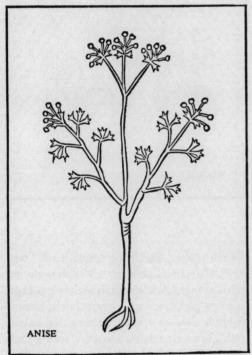

ANISE

sinthe. In Latin countries, especially, the seeds flavor bread, rolls, and cookies. Anise appears in the *U.S. Pharmacopoeia* as a flavoring in medicines, notably paregoric.

Basil   Ocimum Basilicum, L.

Basil added flavor to many a mediaeval dish. In a fifteenth-century manuscript it is included among the herbs to be grown "for potage." In *The Goodman of Paris* it appears in a recipe for "green pickle" along with hyssop, clary, marjoram, and sorrel.

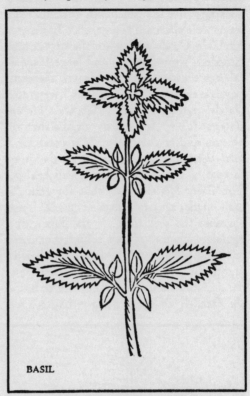

BASIL

Dioscorides warns against eating too much of it since it "dulls the eyesight" and is "hard of digestion." A strange use for basil is indicated in the following excerpt from a mediaeval manuscript: "To make a woman shall not eat of anything that is set on the table, take a little green basil and when the dishes are brought to the table, put it underneath them that the woman perceive it not, for men say that she will eat none of that which is on the dish whereunder the basil lieth." ℂ Basil is a popular flavoring herb today, especially in tomato dishes. It appears in modern recipes for turtle soup and oxtail soup and it is good in omelettes and salads.

Bay, Sweet   Laurus nobilis, L.

In the Middle Ages bay leaves flavored soups, meat jellies, and wines. Bay leaves boiled in water with orange peel made a washing-water for "the hands at table." The leaves were also used as a garnish. In a menu from *The Goodman of Paris* the first course included "cooked apples and large Provençal figs roasted, with bay leaves thereon." Bay leaves "being well smelling" were also "layde amonge clothes." *Banckes's Herbal* states that bay "is good to purge a man of phlegm and of the choler. It is good for a man that may not hear, for if the juice thereof be put in his ears...it will heal it." The *Grete Herball* adds that for colic "a bath made of bay leaves is good." Also "against the evil color of the face...and against a manner of red things that come in young folks faces...take new bay berries and put out the hulks and make fine powder and put it in honey and anoint or bathe the face." ☾ In modern times bay is used for flavoring soups, sauces, meats, game, and fish, as well as most pickles sold on the market.

BORAGE

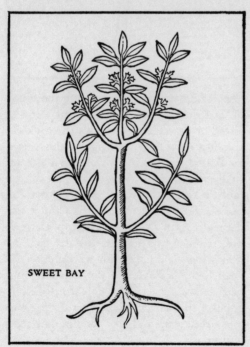

SWEET BAY

Borage   Borago officinalis, L.

When cooked the young leaves made "porray" or greens. The fresh leaves were an important ingredient in salads with mints, sage, parsley, garlic, fennel, rosemary. The beautiful blue flowers were sometimes used to garnish custards, salads, and even soups. Borage was good for healing as well. *Banckes's Herbal* states that it "will cleanse the red choler of a man" and will destroy abscesses "that be gathered of the black choler." Also, "the water drunk with wine maketh a man glad and merry." Many writers refer to the cheering, invigorating effect of this herb. ☾ Fresh borage is used today for imparting a cucumber flavor to salads and cold drinks. In France a tisane of the leaves and flowers is much esteemed for feverish colds. Bees like the flowers, and in some parts of this country borage is grown in large quantities as a honey crop.

Caraway   Carum Carvi, L.

Many a mediaeval feast ended with "caraway in comfits." These well-known seeds appear in recipes for preserves along with anise seeds, coriander, and fennel. The leaves were also used for "potage." The medicinal value of caraway is vouched for by Dioscorides, who says that it is "warming" and "good for the stomach." *Banckes's Herbal* adds that it destroys "wicked winds and the cough." It is "good for the frenzy and for biting of venomous beasts. Also it restoreth hair where it has fallen away." ℂ Caraway seeds are widely used today as flavoring for bread, cakes, confectionery, and so forth;

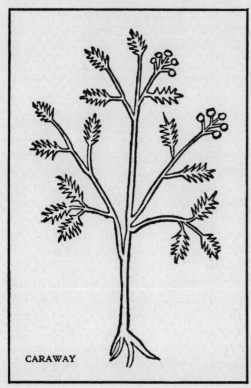

CARAWAY

the oil plays an important part in the distilling of liqueurs such as kümmel. It appears in the *U. S. Pharmacopoeia* as a flavoring for purgatives.

CLARY

Clary   Salvia Sclarea, L.

Clary, sometimes called "Oculus Christi," is one of the familiar potherbs of the Middle Ages. When "put in pottage it will make the flesh tender," claims a mediaeval herbal. In *The Goodman of Paris* it appears among the ingredients for herb omelette and in a recipe for "green pickle for preserving fish." Clary is included also among "herbez for the coppe [cup]" in a fifteenth-century manuscript. A slightly later manuscript states: "Some brewers of ale doe put it in their drink to make it more heady, fit to please drunkards." The seeds were good for "sickness of the eyes." ℭ Clary is now grown commercially in Europe for its oil, which has an odor like lavender and is used as a fixative in perfume. Clary wine made of the clary plant in flower is said to be delicious.

Coriander   Coriandrum sativum, L.

Coriander seeds were used in the Middle Ages to flavor wines, preserves, and even soups and meat. One delectable dish of fowl and veal cooked with bacon in water and wine was powdered with "a spice that is hight red coriander" and garnished with "pomegranate seeds and fried almonds." The herbalist states that the seeds are "good to do away with the fevers that come the third day" and when "drunken with honey" will slay worms. ℭ It is grown today as a flavoring for curry powder, frankfurters, pickles, and some liqueurs but is used in medicines only because of its pleasant taste. Coriander is mentioned in the *U.S. Pharmacopoeia*.

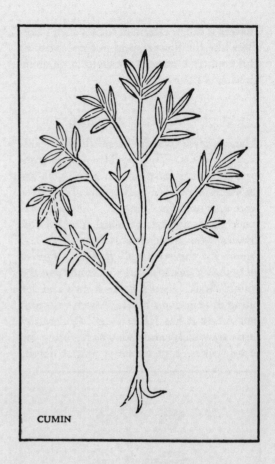

CUMIN

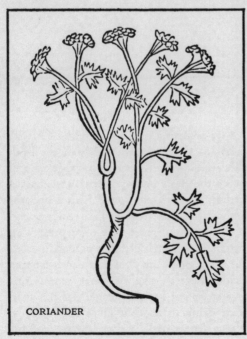

CORIANDER

Cumin   Cuminum Cyminum, L.

In biblical times the Pharisees paid tithes of cumin, and in mediaeval England the vassals sometimes gave cumin seeds as quit-rents in lieu of feudal services. Cumin was a popular spice for fowl; *The Goodman of Paris* gives a recipe for chicken cooked in water and wine, then fried, and cut up fine with ginger, verjuice, saffron, and cumin, calling this "Comminée de Poulaille." Cumin sometimes flavored that aristocrat of dishes, roasted peacock. "Its virtue," says *Banckes's Herbal*, "is to destroy wicked winds and other evils in a man's stomach." ℭ Cumin is now used in curry powder, sauerkraut, German breadstuffs and certain liqueurs, notably kümmel.

Dill   Anethum graveolens, L.

Dill was grown as a potherb in the Middle Ages. It was also listed along with gilly-flower, sweet marjoram, garlic, and others among the "herbes for savour and beauty." *Banckes's Herbal* testifies to the medicinal value of this plant. "It assuageth rumbling in a man's womb [stomach] and wicked winds in the womb. Also, it destroyeth the yexing [hiccups]. The seed of this herb burnt and laid upon a wound, it healeth soon." ⟨ Dill is best known today as a flavoring for cucumber pickles. It is said to be good in boiled cabbage, turnips, and cauliflower. "Dill Water" appears in the *British Pharmacopoeia* as a mild stomach medicine for children.

DILL

Dittany of Crete   Origanum Dictamnus, L.

This is probably the dittany mentioned in Charlemagne's list of herbs. It is used in one mediaeval recipe with rue, pepper, parsley, and garlic as a "pepper sauce" for fish and, in another, as one of fifteen herbs for an herb omelette. The mediaeval herbals state that it had the property of drawing "a thorn or an iron out of a man's body." ⟨ Dittany is an important ingredient in vermouth and is good as a flavoring in salads. The plant is comparatively rare in this country. Fraxinella *(Dictamnus albus, L.)*, also sometimes known as dittany, is more common.

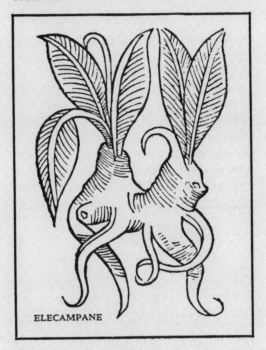

ELECAMPANE

Elecampane   Inula Helenium, L.

A fourteenth-century cookbook tells how to make a sweetmeat of the roots of elecampane. "Take elena campana and seethe it in water. Take it up and grind it well in a mortar. Temper it with eggs, saffron and salt and do it over the fire and let it not boil. Cast above powder douce [probably sugar and spices] and serve it forth." "The virtue of this herb is thus," states *Banckes's*

Herbal: "If a man have wagging teeth and eat of this herb, they shall fasten again." It is also "good for the cough." ℭ Elecampane root is still used in Europe for whooping cough, bronchitis, and asthma. In this country it is employed by veterinary doctors in the treatment of horses. (A common name for elecampane in the Middle Ages was "horseheal.") It is an ingredient in absinthe and in a special aromatic wine produced in Alsace.

Fennel   Foeniculum vulgare, Mill.

Many were the uses of fennel. The seeds flavored sweets, sauces for fish, sausages, and soups. For a "cold brewit [broth]... take pulp of almonds, dry it in a cloth and when it is dried put it in a vessel; add thereto salt, sugar, and white powder of ginger and juice of fennel with wine." Fennel seed boiled in new wine and then dried gave the final touch to a dish of choke-pears in *The Goodman of Paris.* Cooked with pars-

ley and beet greens the leaves made a good "porray"; raw, they were an important ingredient in a green salad. Mediaeval herbalists state that fennel seed "comforteth the stomach." "Also, if it be drunken with wine, it will break the dropsy, and all manner swelling." It was good for mistiness of the eyes and worms in the ears. It made "a woman's milk to increase." ℭ Fennel is still used as a flavoring for fish sauces, salads, soups, and certain drinks. It also appears in the *U. S. Pharmacopoeia* as an important ingredient in laxatives.

HYSSOP

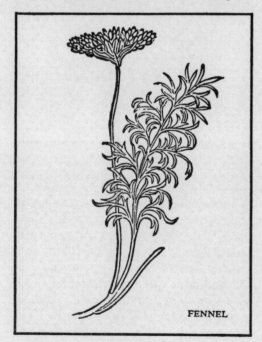

FENNEL

Hyssop   Hyssopus officinalis, L.

Many plants have been called "hyssop," and the hyssop of the Bible is now supposed to have been one of the marjorams. In the Middle Ages hyssop added a bitter taste to soups, pickles, meat pies, and poultry stuffings. One recipe for broth says: "Take parsley and hyssop and sage and hack it small and boil it in wine and in water and a little powder of pepper and mess it forth." In a fifteenth-century manuscript, it is included among "Herbes for the Coppe." *Banckes's Herbal* states that the juice of hyssop "will heal all manner evils of the mouth." It "slayeth worms in a man." "Also, if it be drunken green or in powder, it maketh a man well-coloured." ℂ Hyssop still plays a part in modern European cookery and is an ingredient in many liqueurs such as Chartreuse.

Mallows   Althaea officinalis, L. (ill.)
AND MALVA SYLVESTRIS, L.

Mallows were among the common potherbs of the Middle Ages, along with beets, clary, and so forth. A plaster made of mallow and sheep's tallow was good for the gout. "Sodden with vinegar and linseed," it helped "the wicked gatherings that be engendered in a man's body." Moreover, it kept witches away from one's house. ℂ Country people of Europe and Asia still cook the roots and

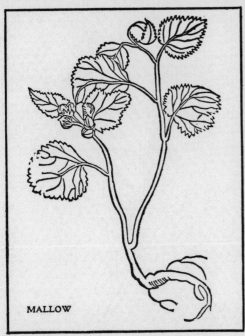

MALLOW

foliage of mallow as a vegetable and sometimes add the young green tops to salads. Lozenges for sore chests and soothing poultices for inflamed skins are made of this herb. French babies are given mallow roots to chew on as an aid in cutting teeth. The root of *Athaea officinalis* is included as an emollient in the *U. S. Pharmacopoeia*.

MARIGOLD

Marigold   Calendula officinalis, L.

The flowers of the marigold, either fresh or dried, gave color and flavor to mediaeval soups and drinks. They were also considered to have great potency in medicine. Even to look on marigolds would draw "evil humours" out of the head and strengthen the eyesight. The marigold was of value against "the pestilence," poisoning, intestinal trouble, scabs on the head, and angry words. The *Grete Herball* states that "maidens make garlands of it when they go to feasts or bridals because it hath fair yellow flowers and ruddy." ℂ In more recent times, marigold lotions and ointments have been used for sprains, wounds, and skin affections. The petals are good in soups.

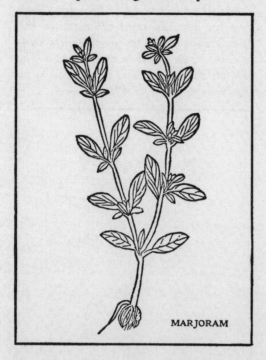

MARJORAM

Marjorams   Origanum vulgare, L.

AND MAJORANA HORTENSIS, MOENCH.
Marjoram was a "must" in every mediaeval garden. It was used to flavor soups, meat dishes, omelettes, pickles, salads. According to Crescentius, it had "a noble taste." In the brewing of ale and beer, marjoram took the place of hops before hops were "discovered." It is found in French recipes for preparing "hippocras," an elaborate spiced wine. Sweet marjoram made a good water for hand washing at meals. The herb bound on the head would cure a cold; drunk with wine, it warmed the stomach, comforting digestion. It was grown for its "savour and beauty." ⪫ Marjoram is used by good cooks of many lands today as an excellent flavoring in stuffings, salads, and soups. Oil distilled from the plant is an important ingredient in certain perfumes.

Mints   Mentha aquatica, L.;

M. CRISPA, TER.; M. PIPERITA, L.; M. ROTUNDIFOLIA, HUDS.; M. SPICATA, L.; AND M. SYLVESTRIS, L.
There are as many varieties of mint, says a ninth-century writer, as there are sparks from Vulcan's furnace, and there were about as many uses for mint in the Middle Ages as there were species. It is mentioned in countless recipes for meat dishes, omelettes, and salads. It was strewn on floors and in the streets of cities for triumphal entries. *Banckes's Herbal* describes how, rubbed on the teeth, it will give "a sweet-smelling mouth"; made into a sauce, "it will make thee to have a talent [appetite] to thy meat"; used as a poultice, it will cure "botches on the face." Mint is good for the toothache; it is used to prevent vomiting. "If it be oft eaten, it will slay worms." ⪫ Mints are cultivated in large quantities today for sauces and drinks, candy and chewing gum, tooth-

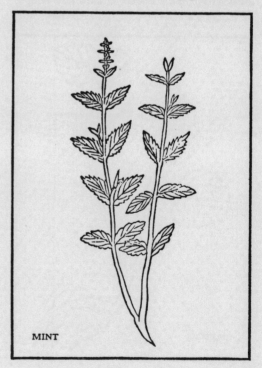

MINT

paste and remedies for indigestion. Peppermint and spearmint are in the *U. S. Pharmacopoeia*.

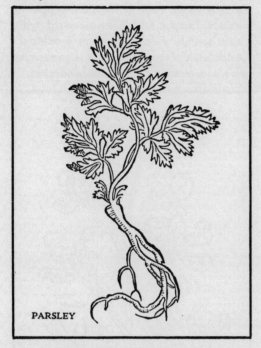

PARSLEY

Parsley   Petroselinum crispum, Nym.

Parsley was "good in pottage and to stop [stuff] chickens." For an "improvised soup," says *The Goodman of Paris,* "take parsley and fry it in butter, then pour boiling water on to it and boil it and add salt and serve your sops." Parsley was also an important ingredient in herb omelettes, green pickles, and nearly every mediaeval dish that called for herbs. It was, even in those days, used as a garnish. *Banckes's Herbal* states that "it multiplieth greatly a man's blood....It is good for the side and the dropsy. It comforteth the heart and the stomach." (We still garnish food with parsley and eat it because of the vitamins. Parsley is used for soups and stews and herb omelettes, much as in the Middle Ages. It is one herb that everyone knows.

Peony   Paeonia officinalis, L.

Peony seeds were used as a spice in foods. The Alewife in *Piers Plowman* says: "I have pepper and peony seed and a pound of garlic and a farthingworth of fennel seed for fasting days." According to *Banckes's Herbal,* peony is "good for women for diverse sickness. Peony seed when it is black, it maketh deliverance...of the child in her womb, and at every time when she shall use to drink it, she must drink fifteen seeds at one time." The root was used as a cure for palsy and lunacy. "Also, for a man or woman that hath the falling evil [epilepsy], eat it and drink it with wine, also hang the root about his neck and it will save him without doubt within fifteen days." Some writers assert that the peony will guard against storms and devils and nightmares and fears. It was sometimes known as the "blessed rose." (The mediaeval virtues of peonies seem not to be recognized today.

PEONY

Primrose & Cowslip

Primula vulgaris, L.
AND P. VERIS, L. (ILL.)

Primrose leaves were used as potherbs in the Middle Ages and "Primerose buddus" as an ingredient in salads. A dish called a "primrose" was made of "flour of rice, 3 pounds of almonds, half an ounce of honey and saffron and the flowers of primrose," tempered with almond milk and dusted with powdered ginger. "Also, the juice put in a man's nose will destroy the megrim," says *Banckes's Herbal*. The cowslip was often called "herba paralysis" because it was believed to be "good for the palsy and gouty folk and them that fall of the high evil called epilepsy." *The vertuose boke of distyllacyon* states that the distilled water from the leaves and flowers of the cowslip "is good against the pain in the head coming of cold," "biting of mad dogs," and "for women that beareth child." Also, "the face often washed therewith withdraweth the spots and pimples in the face and causeth the skin to be fair." ℭ Country people in northern Europe still make a cowslip wine which herbalists recommend as a sedative. An infusion of primrose root is sometimes taken as a remedy for nervous headaches.

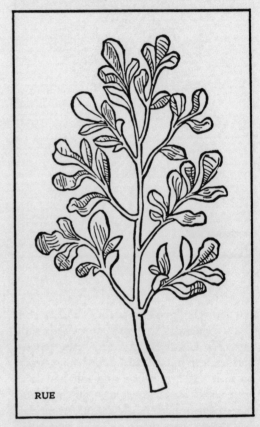

RUE

COWSLIP

Rue

Ruta graveolens, L.

Rue, though bitter, was often used in the Middle Ages as a seasoning for salads, herb omelettes, and sauces for fish. Since it appears among herbs "for the coppe" in a fifteenth-century manuscript, it probably also flavored wines and beers. It was considered of value as an antidote to ward off disease, insects, witches, and all manner of evil things. It was known as the herb of grace. "For the disease which is called lethargy, and in our language is denominated forgetfulness," says Pseudo-Apuleius, "take the wort Rue, washed in vinegar, souse then the forehead therewith." *Banckes's Herbal* recommends it for headache, "stopping of the spleen and the liver," poisoning, and snake bites. "Also, for feebleness of sight put rue in a pot with ale and let the patient use to drink of it." ⁋ Rue is one of the herbs in "aromatic vinegar" and is sometimes added by Italians to salads. Country people of Europe put rue in their beds to get rid of bugs and hang sprigs of it in their houses to keep away flies.

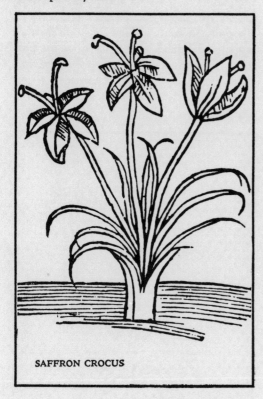

SAFFRON CROCUS

Saffron Crocus   Crocus sativus, L.

About one-third of all the mediaeval recipes for the well-to-do households call for saffron. One says vehemently: "For hen in broth, color it with saffron for Goddes sake." This herb added a distinctive flavor as well as a golden yellow color. It is said that Henry VIII was so fond of it in his food that he forbade the use of it by court ladies for hair dye. Since only the stigmas are used, it takes about 75,000 flowers to make one pound. *Banckes's Herbal* claims that saffron "will destroy all manner of abomination of man's stomach and will make a man sleep." ⁋ Saffron is now too expensive to be used for coloring alone. It is valued as a distinctive scent in oriental types of perfume, and as a flavor for certain foods, especially in Spain. Many mothers give saffron tea in cases of measles, believing that it will bring out the rash.

Sage   Salvia officinalis, L.

Sage was well at the top of any mediaeval list of herbs. It was grown "for potage," for salads, for "Pig in Sawce Sage," for poultry stuffings and meat pies. For "chickens in hocchee," says the *Forme of Cury*, "take chickens and scald them. Take parsley and sage without any other herbs. Take garlic and grapes and stop the chickens full and seethe them in good broth...and mess them forth." *The Goodman of Paris* describes how to make sage water for hand washing at meals, how to flavor white wine with sage, ginger, and bay leaves, and how to cure a toothache by breathing the steam of boiling water into which "sage and other herbs" have been "set." It was considered good for the general health. "Why should a man die whilst sage grows in his garden?" is a much-quoted mediaeval saying. Sage soothed the nerves, quieted the shaking of the palsy, improved digestion. "Also," says *Banckes's Herbal*, "it is good for venom or poison. Seethe sage in ale or wine and use to drink

SAGE

Savories were included in mediaeval dishes when a rather "peppery" flavor was desired. For goose with "Sauce Madame," says the *Forme of Cury,* "take sage, parsley, hyssop and savory, quinces and pears, garlic and grapes and fill the geese therewith and sew the hole that no grease come out and roast it well...." "It is forbidden to use it much in meats," says *Banckes's Herbal,* since it "stirreth him that useth lechery." If it was drunk in wine, however, it would "make thee a good meek stomach." Crescentius recommends it as a purgative, as a remedy in complaints of the liver and lungs, and as a bleach for tanned complexions. ⟪ Savory is a popular seasoning today for poultry, sausages, and boiled fish. It is good in pea soup. Summer savory is called *Bohnenkraut* (bean herb) in Germany because it is an essential flavoring in a pottage made of beans and meat.

SAVORY

it three days, and thou shall be whole, by the grace of God....Also, if a man have an itching, wash the itching well with the juice of this herb and it shall slay the itching soon....Who that useth to eat of this herb or drink it, it is marvel that any inconvenience should grieve them." ⟪ Sage ranks first among seasoning herbs in the United States today. It is the right seasoning for pork, especially pork sausage, and is good in cheese, poultry stuffing, and baked fish. A hot drink of sage and milk is enjoyed by Hollanders after winter skating and sage tea with sugar and lemon or lime is considered by some people to be very refreshing. Italian peasants still eat the fresh leaves to preserve their health and country folk of many lands administer sage tea as a remedy for weak stomachs and nervous headaches, fevers and colds.

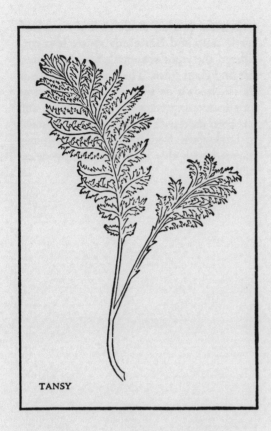

TANSY

Tarragon　Artemisia Dracunculus, L.

Mediaeval references to the use of tarragon are very rare. Ibn Baithar, physician and botanist, who lived in Spain in the thirteenth century, says that the tender tops of tarragon were cooked with vegetables, and that tarragon juice was used to flavor drinks. He wrote further that it sweetened the breath, dulled the taste of bitter medicine, and put one to sleep. ⫸ Tarragon is used today more widely than in the Middle Ages. Its leaves, fresh or dried, are good in salads, and tarragon vinegar is considered by many people an essential ingredient in French dressing. Sauces for fish are often flavored with tarragon; Sauce Béarnaise and Sauce Tartare require it.

Thymes　Thymus Serpyllum, L. (ill.)
AND T. VULGARIS, L.

Thyme was grown in many a mediaeval garden as an herb "for potage." Dioscorides says: "Being eaten with meat it avails for

THYME

Tansy　Tanacetum vulgare, L.

The young leaves of tansy mixed with eggs was known as a "tansy." At Easter time, it was a favorite dish eaten to celebrate the end of Lent. Also, it was believed to be of value in purifying the "bad humours" of the body after the long diet of salt fish. "Tansy is good *hot*," states an English book of manners. In a fifteenth-century manuscript it is included among the "herbez to stylle [distill]." It is one of several herbs in a fourteenth-century prescription for cure of the plague. ⫸ The flavor of tansy is too strong for most modern palates. Country people, however, still use tansy tea for relieving stomach cramps and for expelling worms in children. Physicians claim that it has no medicinal value and warn against the use of it in large quantities.

the dull sighted. It is good instead of sauce for the use in health." He prescribes it mixed with honey for driving out "phlegmy matter from the thorax, for asthma and for expelling worms." Crescentius adds that if you "drink the wine in which the herb has been cooked, it will warm the heart, the liver and the spleen." ℭ As a flavoring, however, thyme is probably more popular now than it was in the Middle Ages. It is used largely for poultry stuffings and meat loaf, turtle soup and Burgundy sauce. It is considered the right seasoning for clam chowder and clam juice. The active principle of its oil, known as thymol, is recognized as an effective ingredient in cough drops and has been used with success in the treatment of hookworm. Bees love thyme, and honey flavored with this herb is especially delectable.

Herbs for Healing

A Sick Man in Bed from Brunschwig's LIBER DE ARTE DISTILLANDI,
Strassburg, Grüninger, 1500

Agrimony   Agrimonia Eupatoria, L.

This herb, "being beaten small when it is green," says Dioscorides, "hath power to cure cuts." *Banckes's Herbal* states that it is especially good "to heal a wound that is hurt with iron." It was likewise used for many ills, such as "inflammation of the eyes, aching of the womb, bites of poisonous beasts, convulsions, warts, and absent-mindedness." "For sleeplessness," writes Crescentius, "bathe the feet in the water in which it was cooked. It helps." ☾ Modern official medicine does not recognize these virtues. Since agrimony contains a certain amount of tannin, however, modern herbalists feel justified in recommending its use as a home remedy for cuts and wounds even as in the Middle Ages. A decoction of the leaves mixed with honey and syrup of mulberries is said to make an effective gargle for coughs and sore throats. The whole plant yields a fine yellow dye.

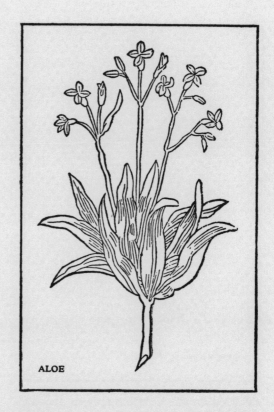

ALOE

AGRIMONY

Aloe   Aloe vera, L.

Dioscorides mentions the bitter taste of aloes. He then describes at great length the value of aloe juice, from the "conglutinating of wounds" and "loosening of the belly" to "procuring sleep" and preventing "the hair falling off." The *Grete Herball* adds that this herb is good "for worms in the belly and ears" and for "ill color caused of the coldness of the stomach." ☾ Aloes appear in the *U. S. Pharmacopoeia* as a cathartic. Recently, the fresh leaves of this plant have assumed importance in curing X-ray and radium burns that do not respond to any other treatment.

Balm, Lemon   Melissa officinalis, L.

Dioscorides says that the leaves of balm "being drunk with wine and also applied,

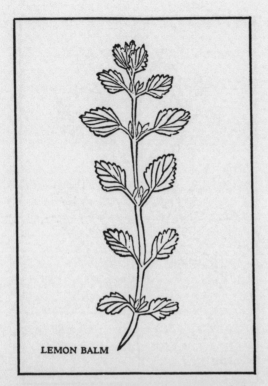

LEMON BALM

Betony was a sovereign remedy for many ills in the Middle Ages. "It is good whether for the man's soul or for his body," says an early mediaeval herbal. "It shields him against monstrous nocturnal visitors and against frightful visions and dreams....If a man become tired in mickle riding or in mickle goings let him take betony...seethe it in sweetened wine; drink at night fasting three cups full; then he will soon be un-weary." *Banckes's Herbal* states that if betony "be stamped and then laid to a wound in the head...it will heal the wound fair." It is good for all diseases of the head, for watery eyes, aching ears, bleeding at the nose, toothache, and the cough. Also, "take and eat betony...and you shall not be drunken that day. All these medicines [cures] have been proved of this herb." The *Grete Herball* adds that powder of betony in warm water and wine will cure "them that be too

are good for the Scorpion-smitten and the dog-bitten. Being smeared on they will assuage the pains of the gout." The *Grete Herball* claims that "meddled with grease" balm is good against all aches. Also, "the wine that melissa is sodden in is good to keep one from swooning if the cause be cold." "The dried leaves laid on top of the head will draw out the congestion and leave one light-headed," the *Hortus sanitatis* asserts. "The leaves taken with salt and eaten will relieve the difficulty in breathing...and will clear the chest." It also "helpeth conception more." ℭ In European countries, balm is still used as a home remedy for fainting and dizziness, for wounds, neuralgia, and feverish colds. It is an ingredient in Chartreuse, Benedictine, and other liqueurs. The dried leaves add flavor to soups and sauces; the fresh leaves are good in claret cup and other cold beverages made with wine.

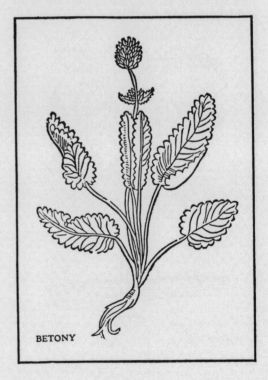

BETONY

fearful" if given "at the time that the fear cometh." ⟨ Unhappily none of these cures is admitted by official medicine today, though betony tea is still taken sometimes as a home remedy for nervous headaches, dyspepsia, and hysteria. Country people of Europe often smoke betony leaves in place of tobacco.

BUGLOSS

Bugloss   Anchusa officinalis, L.

According to the *Hortus sanitatis*, this herb "is good for him who has harmful wicked moistness of the lung" and "a bad cough." "The juice drunk with warm water helps swollen feet," "mixed with wine it develops good blood" and "strengthens the heart." "When laid in wine, then mixed with honey wine and drunk, it makes a man merry and glad." "Also," adds *Banckes's Herbal*, "this herb drunken with hot water maketh a man to have a good mind and good wit." ⟨ It is

a pity that for most of the above purposes bugloss seems unavailing today. The root of bugloss, like its relative Alkanet (*Alkanna tinctoria, Tausch.*), yields a red dye. The leaves and flowers are sometimes used as a home remedy for a cough.

Celandine   Chelidonium majus, L.

Banckes's Herbal, quoting Galen, says that celandine "is good for sore eyes. It is good for the canker in a man's mouth and for him that hath drunken venom." Also, "take selondyne [celandine] and draw out the juice thereof and meddle it with white wine and anoint the visage therewith, and it shall do away freckles of the visage." ⟨ The drug from celandine bears a close resemblance to opium, but is not employed in medicine at the present time. Country folk use the orange-colored juice of this herb to cure warts, ringworm, and corns.

CELANDINE

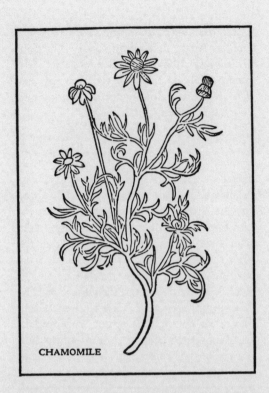

CHAMOMILE

headaches, for run-down systems and pale complexions. Beauty shops of several lands use a chamomile rinse after shampoos, especially for blonde hair.

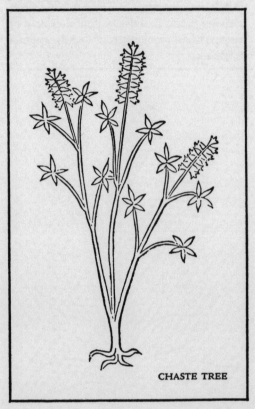

CHASTE TREE

Chamomile Anthemis nobilis, L.
AND MATRICARIA CHAMOMILLA, L.

"The virtue of this herb is thus," claims *Banckes's Herbal,* "if it be drunken with wine, it will break the stone. Also, it destroyeth the yellow evil. It helpeth the aching and disease of the liver. It is good for the aching of a man's head and for the megrim [migraine]." "To take away...kernels that come in the face," adds the *Grete Herball,* "seethe green chamomile with honey and anoint the face therewith." Chamomile flowers boiled with orange peel make a good "water for washing the hands at table," according to *The Goodman of Paris.* It is one of the herbs in John Russell's recipe for "the making of a bathe medicinable." ℂ Although physicians today claim that chamomile has no medicinal value, many a French housewife will administer chamomile tea for weak stomachs and nervous

Chaste Tree Vitex Agnus-castus, L.

According to the *Hortus sanitatis* "the seed, leaves and flowers of this plant when eaten by wicked, unchaste people will make them chaste like lambs." Moreover, "if you strew the leaves and flowers under the bed, you will have in sleep peace from wicked, unchaste dreams." *Banckes's Herbal* adds that the herb will "destroy the dropsy, defy the hardness and stopping of the milt [spleen] and will do away the ache of a man's head that is engendered by wicked humors." ℂ Apparently none of these virtues is recognized at the present time.

Colchicum   Colchicum autumnale, L.

Dioscorides knew only of the poisonous nature of this herb, warning the inexperienced that "it killeth by choking," though it be "strangely alluring" because of its "pleasantness." Later mediaeval herbalists, however, recognized the value of colchicum for "sore of joints" and "all gouts." Pseudo-Apuleius claimed that it was also good "if pimples wax on a woman's face." ⦅ Colchicum appears in the *U.S. Pharmacopoeia* as a remedy for gout and rheumatism. At the present time horticulturists are experimenting with the remarkable effects of colchicine on living plant cells. It is the only drug so far known to produce hereditary change in plants.

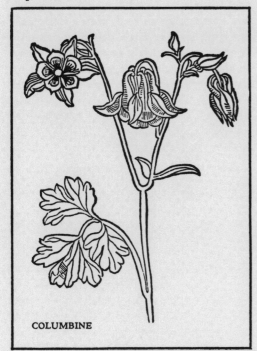

COLUMBINE

Columbine   Aquilegia vulgaris, L.

A fifteenth-century manuscript includes this plant among the "herbs for potage." *Banckes's Herbal* states that "its virtue is good for him that hath the quinsy." Pseudo-Apuleius claims that if "any one have with him this herb…he will not be barked at by dogs." When drunk, "it driveth away all poisons; also, it is said that sorcerers use it for their crafts." A fourteenth-century manuscript lists columbine as one of seven herbs which, "stamped" and drunk with ale, will destroy the pestilence "be it never so fell." ⦅ Columbine has no practical value today.

Cuckoo-Pint   Arum maculatum, L.

Banckes's Herbal states that "if a man have any swelling upon the tongue, or any swelling about his ears, take this herb and seethe it with…wine and oil and with cumin, and make a plaster thereof and lay it to his ears, and it will make him whole." Also "if thou wilt make thy face white and clear, take the powder of the roots and lay it in rose water and set it against the sun till it be consumed. Do so twice or thrice. Then rub thy face

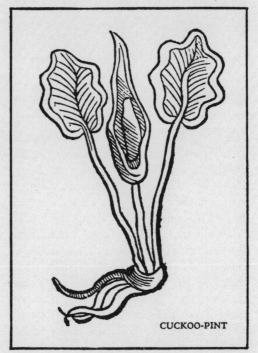

CUCKOO-PINT

with the powder, or what other place thou wilt, to fret away the superfluity of flesh." ℂ Today these virtues seem not to be recognized by anyone.

FEVERFEW

Feverfew   Chrysanthemum Parthenium, Pers.

"Its virtue is to comfort a man's stomach." It is "good to assuage the access [ague], quotidian, cramp" and "to lay to a sore that is bitten by venomous beasts....Also if it be stamped and laid to a wound in which be broken bones, it shall bring the broken bones together and heal them." These claims for the value of "federfoy" are made by *Banckes's Herbal*. The *Hortus sanitatis* states that "the seeds eaten will drive out worms from the body" and "drunk with wine will make a woman fruitful." ℂ Country people of today, especially in Europe, make considerable use of this herb as a tonic for highly

nervous patients and as a cure for cough and colic. In *A Modern Herbal* Grieve states that "a tincture made from feverfew and applied locally, immediately relieves the pain and swelling caused by bites of insects and vermin." But the herb has no official place in modern medicine.

Hemlock, Poison   Conium maculatum, L.

"The juice of this herb," states *Banckes's Herbal*, "keepeth maiden's teats small. Also, this herb oft drunken...destroyeth the great appetite of lechery. Also, the juice tempered with swine's grease destroyeth the hot podagra [gout] and assuageth the great swelling, for it is cold and dry." This is the poison hemlock given to Socrates. ℂ Because the drug from hemlock acts as a paralyser of the nerve centers, it has been widely used in therapeutics until recent times. It is no

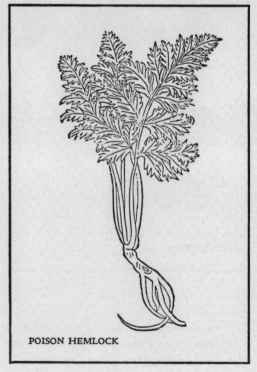

POISON HEMLOCK

longer officially recognized in the pharmacology of the United States, but in Europe it is still employed in external applications to relieve the pain of ulcers, rheumatism, and gout. Hemlock juice is sometimes given internally as a sedative; the drug has also been recommended by herbalists as an antidote to strychnine poisoning.

HOUSELEEK

Houseleek or Hen-and-Chickens   Sempervivum tectorum, L.

This herb, often called "Jupiter's beard" in the Middle Ages, "hath a cooling, binding faculty," says Dioscorides, being good for "inflammation of the eyes, the feet gouts," hemorrhage, and headaches. Crescentius adds that the juice laid on hot ulcers drives away infection and that an ointment of sempervivum juice and the oil of roses is good for burns. "Whosoever is deaf," states the *Hortus sanitatis*, "should take the milk of a woman who nurses a boy ten or twelve weeks old and put with this the juice of the houseleek and then drip three or four drops into the ear soothingly…and the hearing will come back without fail." Houseleeks were often planted on the tiled and thatched roofs of houses in the belief that they warded off lightning. ℂ Today country people sometimes apply the bruised leaves or juice of this herb to burns and scalds for quick relief and to cuts for stanching the flow of blood.

Ivy, Ground   Nepeta hederacea, Trev.

Pseudo-Apuleius explains that earth ivy is good for stones in the bladder, for "sore of milt," and for "bite of creeping things"; also it is used "in case the nostrils smell ill," or "in case a man is not able to hear well," and "that the head may not ache for heat of sun." *Banckes's Herbal* adds that if it "be sodden

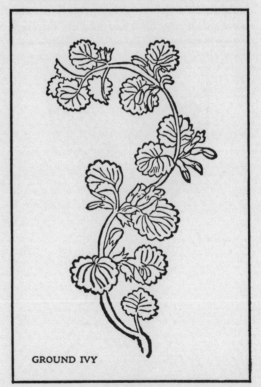

GROUND IVY

in swine's grease, it is good ointment for all manner aches." John Russell includes earth ivy (hey hove) in his "bathe medicinable." This herb was one of those employed in the Middle Ages for flavoring ale before hops were introduced. ℂ Today ground ivy is sometimes administered as a home remedy for coughs and nervous headaches. It has no place in official medicine.

Lily of the Valley · Convallaria majalis, L.

A half-pound of these "sweet smelling flowers" soaked in a liter of wine for four weeks and then distilled, claims the *Hortus sanitatis*, makes a liquor "more precious than gold," for if anyone is troubled with apoplexy, "let him mix the liquor with four peppercorns and a little lavender-water and drink thereof and he shall not have to fear a stroke that month." Moreover, "this wine smeared on the forehead and on the back of the neck makes one to have good common sense." ℂ The drug from the dried rhizome and roots of lily of the valley resembles digitalis and is now sometimes given as a heart tonic.

MANDRAKE

LILY OF THE VALLEY

Mandrake · Mandragora officinarum, L.

The juice of the mandrake root served as an anesthetic in the Middle Ages. Dioscorides describes how it is given to "such as cannot sleep, or are grievously pained, and upon whom being cut or cauterized they [wish to] make a not-feeling pain." He explains that whoever eats of it is "sensible of nothing for three or four hours." The root is also "a maker of love medicines," a cure for apostumes (abscesses), and a softener of ivory. Other herbalists describe the magic potency of mandrake for "devil sickness or insanity," for sterility in women, and for "heavy mischief in the home." One writer claims that it "cures every infirmity—except only death where there is no help." The root was said to bear the likeness of a human form—either male or female—and to screech when being uprooted. Many believed that the person who dug it up would surely die. Consequently elaborate schemes were developed for persuading dogs to perform the job instead. Several mediaeval herbalists question the veracity of many of these statements. For instance, the author of the *Grete Herball* writes as follows: "Some say that the male hath the shape of a man and the female of a woman, but that is false. For nature never gave form or shape of mankind to an herb. But it is of truth that some hath shaped figures by craft as we have foretime heard say." ℭ The drug from the mandrake root is similar to belladonna in its narcotic effects but is little used at the present time.

Myrtle   Myrtus communis, L.

Dioscorides recommends myrtle for many ailments: ulcers, erysipelas, spitting of blood, "joints that are loosened and fractures that are hard to grow together." Also, "being drank before, it doth prevent surfeiting." The "dry leaves being beaten small are profitable strawed [strewn] upon... armpits and thighs that are moist." A decoction of the fruit was good for "the blacking of the hair." ℭ In France the essential oil from the leaves and flowers of myrtle is known as "eau d'anges" and is used in perfume. Certain peoples in southern Europe make of the fermented fruit of myrtle an alcoholic beverage which is said to be very "agreeable to the taste." German brides wear wreaths of myrtle and German grooms put sprigs of myrtle on their coat lapels.

Opium Poppy   Papaver somniferum, L.

Banckes's Herbal speaks of both the white, or opium, poppy and the black, or field, poppy. It says: "For to provoke sleep, make a plaster of each of them or one of them with woman's milk and the white of an egg and lay it to the temples....For fevers, anoint the small of the back with an ointment made of powder of poppy seed and oil of violet heated." "The quantity of a grain...of opium taken in the body," states the *Grete Herball,* "mortifieth all the wits of man in such manner that he feeleth no pain and causeth him to sleep." Crescentius warns that it should be taken cautiously because it "makes you susceptible to colds and can kill you." ℭ Opium is made from the milky juice of the unripe seed capsules of *Papaver somniferum.* Its use today as a hypnotic and sedative is well known. The drugs morphine, codeine, and laudanum, derived from the opium poppy, are official in the *U. S. Pharmacopoeia.*

OPIUM POPPY

PENNYROYAL

be already therein it will be driven out soon. With this herb wicked spirits are cast out of people....And it works much better if the herb is blessed with other herbs on Our Lady's Day." Periwinkle would also "stay the flux," "ease the toothache," and "drive out the wicked fever that comes of severe cold." According to Pseudo-Apuleius it had "good advantage" against snakes and poisons and spite. It helped one to "be happy and comfortable" and "to have grace." ☾ Periwinkle tea is sometimes given today as a home remedy for hemorrhages and inflamed tonsils. It does not appear in official pharmacopoeias.

Pennyroyal — Mentha Pulegium, L.

"If any endure nausea on shipboard," says Pseudo-Apuleius, "let him take the herb pulegium [pennyroyal] and wormwood, let him pound them together with oil and with vinegar and let him smear himself therewith frequently." *Banckes's Herbal* claims that it is good for "cold humor in the head" and "phlegm in the breast," for "an itching boil," "disease in the belly," and "the cramp." ☾ Pennyroyal tea is still used by country folk as a remedy for cramps and colds.

Periwinkle — Vinca minor, L.

This herb, sometimes called "joy of the ground" in the Middle Ages, was endowed with mysterious powers against "wicked spirits." "Whoever carries this herb with him on the skin, the devil has no power over him," states the *Hortus sanitatis*. "No witchery may enter the house which has this herb hanging over the door and if any witchery

PERIWINKLE

Pimpernel — Anagallis arvensis, L.
AND A. A. VAR. CAERULEA

There are two kinds of pimpernel according to the *Hortus sanitatis*: one has "flowers that are of a red color and this is the male; the other has flowers which are sky-colored and that is the female." Blue pimpernel was used in making plasters, and scarlet for sprains. Both were used for "dimness of the eyes, ringing in the ears," and "the swelling that comes with aching of the teeth." When put in the nostrils this herb cleared "the head of wicked dampness." It was good also for "bites of venomous beasts," falling sickness, and "belly ache." ❦ Pimpernel is not recommended for any of these ills today, though pharmacologists recognize the fact that the juice of pimpernel contains a ferment capable of digesting proteins.

it with water, it healeth men that have been bitten by any venomous beast." Also, "this herb destroyeth worms. It is good for the cough and for binding in the belly and in the breast and for the disease in the bones." Furthermore, "this herb burnt and the ashes meddled with oil, it restoreth where any man lacketh hair." The *Hortus sanitatis* adds that "the smoke of this herb will drive away snakes from the house. It has a good smell." ❦ It is said that young country boys still use an ointment made of ashes of southernwood for growing beards. The French call the plant *garderobe*, believing that it will protect clothes from moths and other insects.

Spurge   Euphorbia Lathyrus, L.

This herb has the power of "purging the belly." Since it was very drastic in its effects, the mediaeval herbalists suggested that it be eaten well chopped with wine or served with "an hen or pot herbs." It was a cure for

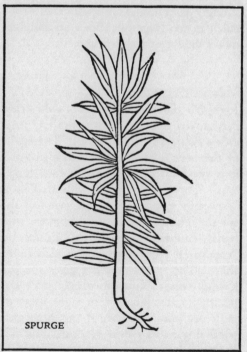

SPURGE

SOUTHERNWOOD

Southernwood   Artemisia Abrotanum, L.

Southernwood seems to have cured many diseases in the Middle Ages. *Banckes's Herbal* states, "The virtue of this herb is thus, that if they break the seed and drink "choler" and "melancholia." Called "cata-pucé" by Chaucer, spurge was recommended to Chanticleer in *The Nun's Priest's Tale* as one of the laxatives to prevent bad dreams. ℭ Spurge is little used today as a cathartic because of the violence of its action. In *A Modern Herbal* Grieve states that the juice of the leaves will raise blisters on the skin and for this reason has been employed by beggars to excite pity.

Stramonium or Thornapple   Datura Stramonium, L.

Dioscorides says of stramonium: "The root being drank with wine the quantity of a drachma hath the power to effect not un-pleasant fantasies. But two drachmas being drank make one beside himself for three days; and four being drank, kill him." ℭ To-day stramonium leaves are official in all pharmacopoeias. The drug, which is of great value in the treatment of asthma, is strongly narcotic and antispasmodic. When taken in too large quantities, stramonium causes giddiness and delirium.

Strawberry, Wild   Fragaria vesca, L.

In the Middle Ages the leaves of wild straw-berries were believed to have healing prop-erties. *Banckes's Herbal* states: "The virtue of this herb is good for bleared men. Also, it is good to destroy the web in a man's eyes." The *Grete Herball* adds that it is "especially good against all evils of the spleen. The juice thereof, drunken with honey, profiteth marvellously." Besides, it "comforteth the stomach and quencheth the thirst." The *Hortus sanitatis* gives the fol-lowing recipe: "Take strawberry juice and plantain water mixed with eight liters of mulberry juice, one liter of the dung of a white dog...and a little vinegar...and this is good for ulcers of the throat if used as

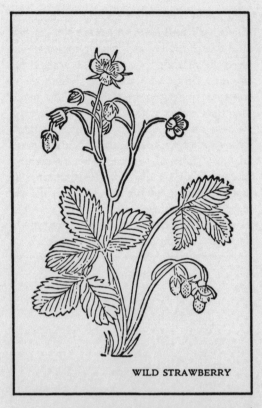

WILD STRAWBERRY

a gargle." Also, "strawberry water is good for those people who sweat too much." ℭ Modern herbalists say that strawberry-leaf tea makes a refreshing beverage and that the fresh fruit will remove discolora-tion of the teeth and whiten the skin.

Vervain   Verbena officinalis, L.

Vervain was considered good for the stom-ach, the liver, and the lungs, "and for them that have the stone." It was taken internally and applied externally in cases of "biting of venomous beasts." It had virtue against "the bark of hound," fevers, and "all poi-sons." For him "that useth it, it will make a good breath." There were its magic prop-erties also: "If one goes to battle, let him seek the vervain and keep it in his clothes and he will escape from his enemies. They that bear vervain upon them shall have love and grace of great masters." Also, "to make folk merry at the table, take four leaves and four roots of vervain in wine; then sprinkle the wine all about the house where the eating is and they shall be all merry." It was called a "holy herb." ⁋ The use of this

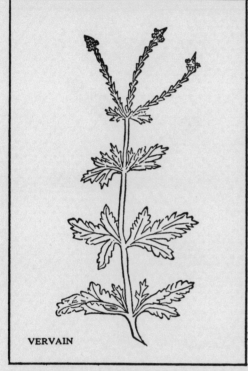

VERVAIN

herb has diminished greatly since the Middle Ages. However, a tisane of vervain is sometimes given for headaches and fevers, and poultices of vervain are applied for ear neuralgia and rheumatic pains.

Wallflower   Cheiranthus Cheiri, L.

This is one of the plants known in the Middle Ages as gillyflower. "The flowers smell like violets," the *Hortus sanitatis* states, "and the lemon-colored ones are the best in medicine." "Juice of the flowers put in the eyes takes away the wicked specks therein."

WALLFLOWER

Water of the distilled flowers "drunk noon and night for three or four weeks doth cause women to be fruitful." It is good also for hard labor in childbirth, paralysis, dropsy, and "the chaps which are in the seat." ⁋ No such cures are claimed for wallflowers at the present time. Though pharmacologists recognize their inclusion in the digitalis series, they are little used as a drug today. They still "smell like violets."

Wormwood Artemisia Absinthium, L.

The juice of the bitter wormwood "mingled with sweet milk is good for worms in the womb" and for "worms in a man's ears," states *Banckes's Herbal*. When drunk with spikenard "it assuageth the wicked winds" of the stomach. "Pounded with the gall of a bull, and afterward put into a man's eyes, it putteth away all manner impediments of the sight. It is good to comfort the heart." ⁋ Wormwood is the base for absinthe and

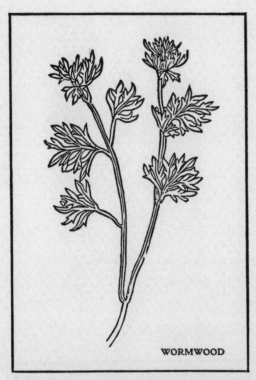

WORMWOOD

was used to stanch the flow of blood both on the battlefield and in the home. Made into a plaster, it was also considered a cure for "the headache"; drunk with "wine or good ale," it stopped "the heartburning." "Also, for him that may not hold his meat [let him] stamp this herb with wine and drink it warm." ❧ Yarrow has no official

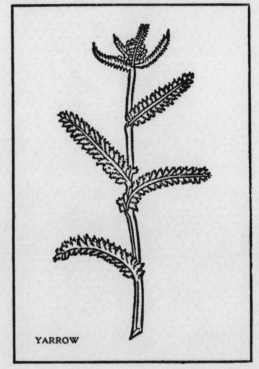

YARROW

is used today in various other liqueurs. It acts very powerfully on the nerve centers, causing hallucinations, delirium, and, in some cases, insanity.

Yarrow   Achillea Millefolium, L.

"King Achilles found this herb," states *Banckes's Herbal,* "and with it he healed his men that were wounded with iron. For wounds, stamp this herb with swine's grease and plaster it to the wound, and it shall heal it." Throughout the Middle Ages yarrow

place in modern medicine. However, the tradition of its value in healing wounds has lingered on in some places, and herbalists recommend yarrow tea as a good remedy for severe colds.

Herbs for Poisoning Pests

"Cleansing the Scalp" from HORTUS SANITATIS, Mainz, Meydenbach, 1491

Aconite or Monkshood — Aconitum Napellus, L.

The root was used as a poison for killing pests. To get rid of rats, *The Goodman of Paris* advises: "Make cakes of paste and toasted cheese and powdered aconite and set these near to their holes where…[the rats] have naught to drink." ℭ Although a deadly poison when taken in large doses, aconite is used by physicians as a cardiac depressant. It has been omitted, however, from the latest edition (1942) of the *U. S. Pharmacopoeia*.

"For killing wolves and foxes," says *The Goodman of Paris,* "take the root of black hellebore and dry the root thoroughly and not in the sun…and with this powder mix ⅕ part of glass well ground and ¼ part of lily leaf. Take honey and fresh fat…and mix them with the aforesaid powder and make it into a hard stiff paste, rolling it into round balls the size of a hen's egg." Dioscorides describes hellebore as a purgative, adding that it is "good for ye Epileptical, Melancholicall, Frantic, Arthriticall, Paralyticall." The *Grete Herball* claims that it will cure gout, "scruff of the head," and scabies. ℭ Though pharmacologists include hellebore in the digitalis series, the plant is grown today mainly because it is one of the earliest blooms in the garden.

Stavesacre or Larkspur — Delphinium Staphisagria, L.

The main use for this herb in the Middle Ages was to get rid of head lice. Crescentius says: "The seed made into a powder and mixed with vinegar is a good salve for lice and scabs. That is why it is called lousewort….Also the powder taken in honey kills worms." "It has great results," claims this writer. ℭ A preparation of stavesacre seeds is still a recognized vermicide for head lice today.

LARKSPUR

Sweet Smelling Herbs

FOR LAYING AMONG CLOTHES AND FOR DIVERS OTHER USES

"Of Lovely, Sweet Scents," woodcut by Weiditz from Petrarch's VON DER ARTZNEY BAYDER GLÜCK, Augsburg, H. Steiner, 1532

Costmary — Chrysanthemum Balsamita, L.

The leaves of this plant are very fragrant and were probably among the sweet herbs used in the Middle Ages for strewing on floors and for scenting the washing-water at meals. Though bitter to taste, costmary appears occasionally in mediaeval books of cookery. It was grown especially, however, as an herb "for the Coppe" and was sometimes called "alecost" because of its importance in flavoring ale and beer. ⟨ Dried costmary with lavender makes a good sachet for perfuming linens. Some people like costmary tea.

Iris — Iris florentina, L.

AND I. GERMANICA, L.

The "well-scenting" roots of iris, says Dioscorides, have a warming faculty, fitting against coughs and convulsions. They help "such as are chilled and stiff with cold." They are good for the "bites of venomous beasts" and "sun burning" and are "causers of sleep and provokers of tears and heal the torments of the belly....In general they are of very much use." Crescentius adds that the root when powdered is soothing to the flesh and that the same mixed with rose water is good for sore eyes. The petals of purple iris, combined with alum, made a beautiful green pigment for painters of mediaeval manuscripts. The "well-scenting" roots produced a delicate perfume. ⟨ Orris-root from *Iris florentina* or *Iris germanica* is used today in perfumes, sachet powders, potpourris, and tooth powders.

LAVENDER

IRIS

Lavenders — Lavandula officinalis, Lois.

AND L. STOÈCHAS, L. (ILL.)

Lavender was an herb highly treasured in the Middle Ages. It perfumed the silks and linens of wealthy folk and was strewn in chests to keep away insects. "The Mother of God" was very fond of lavender flowers, explains the *Hortus sanitatis,* "because of their virtue in protecting clothes from dirty, filthy beasts." She also had "great love of this herb for the reason that it preserves chastity....If the head is sprinkled with lavender water it will make that person chaste as long as he bears it upon him." For a headache the *Hortus* recommends taking the flowers of *Lavandula Stoèchas* and putting them into a little bag along with bay and betony, red roses and marjoram, clove pinks and nutmeg blossoms. "For noblemen" the sack should be made of "red silk" and "for the common people, of plainer stuff." If this little bag is put on the head "it will soothe all pains." Lavender had also "strange, unspeakable virtue" against apoplexy and palsy and loss of speech. ℂ The use of lavender in soaps, perfumes, and sachets is well known today. *A Modern Herbal* states that "in hysteria, palsy and similar disorders...lavender will act as a powerful stimulant." It appears in the *U. S. Pharmacopoeia* as an ingredient in aromatic spirits of ammonia and liniment of soft soap.

Lily, Madonna   Lilium candidum, L.

"The lily is next to the rose in worthiness and nobleness," wrote Bartholomaeus Anglicus, a thirteenth-century scholar. "Nothing is more gracious than the lily in fairness of color, in sweetness of smell and in effect of working and virtue." Dioscorides says that the flowers are used to make an ointment for comforting the sinews. The leaves "being applied do help the serpent-bitten"; they are good also for burns, for "old ulcers, and new wounds." If the root is "beaten small with honey, it cleanseth leprosies"; also "it cleareth the faces and makes them without wrinkles." Crescentius adds that it will

MADONNA LILY

"cause the hair to grow in used-up places." As a cosmetic the red, or wild, lily is better than the white, or tame, lily, claims the *Grete Herball,* which recommends this herb "to make a good color in the face" and "to take away over much redness." ℂ Modern medicine does not acknowledge these virtues. Modern herb lore, however, claims that an ointment of lily bulbs will still relieve the pain from burns and scalds, will bring to a head boils and abscesses, and will remove corns.

Rosemary   Rosmarinus officinalis, L.

Rosemary was one of the best loved as well as one of the most useful of all mediaeval garden herbs. It is found in recipes for salads and green sauces for fish and as a flavoring for wine. The boar's head at Christmas was "garlanded with rosemary," and rosemary scented the water for hand washing at meals. *Banckes's Herbal* states that if you "take the flowers and put them in a chest among your clothes or among books, the moths shall not hurt them.... Also take the flowers and make powder thereof and bind it to thy right arm in a linen cloth and it shall make thee light and merry....Also, boil the leaves in white wine and wash thy face therewith...and thou shalt have a fair face. Also, put the leaves under thy bed's head and thou shalt be delivered of all evil dreams....Also, make thee a box of the wood and smell to it and it shall preserve thy youth....And if thou set it in thy garden, keep it honestly for it is much profitable." ℂ Rosemary is still used in salads and fish sauces, in turtle and in oxtail soups. It is the principal ingredient in a skin astringent called Hungary Water which even today "ensures beauty and makes age a mere flight of time." Oil of rosemary appears in the *U. S. Pharmacopoeia* as a perfume.

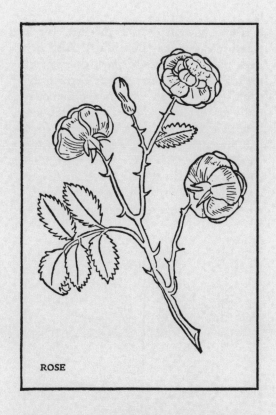

ROSE

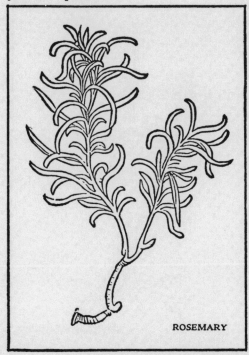

ROSEMARY

Roses   Rosa centifolia, L. (ill.)

R. DAMASCENA, MILL.; R. GALLICA, L., ETC.

To the people of the Middle Ages, the rose was without doubt the "flower of flowers." Rose water was used for hand washing at meals. Dried rose petals were sprinkled among clothes in chests. For this purpose, "the roses of Provins be the best," says *The Goodman of Paris,* "but they must be sifted through a sieve...so that the worms fall through the holes...and after that, spread them over the dresses." In spring, the ladies strewed "their bowers with red roses and lily flowers." Roses, with almonds, sugar, capons, and saffron, made a favorite dish called a "Rosée." Rose sugar was a sweet much prized for parties. *Banckes's Herbal* states that syrup of honey and roses is given to "feeble, sick, phlegmatic, melancholy and choleric people." Rose water is "good for eyes and in ointments of the face, for it taketh away wems [blemishes]. Also dry roses put to the nose to smell do comfort the brain and the heart and quickeneth the spirit." ⌡ Roses are now grown commercially for perfume and hand lotions, for potpourris and sachets. As a flavoring in food and drink, the rose is still popular in some localities, especially in the Near East. *Rosa alba, R. centifolia, R. gallica,* and *R. damascena,* appear in the *U. S. Pharmacopoeia.*

SWEET VIOLET

Violet, Sweet   Viola odorata, L.

"Of all the fragrant herbs I send, none can compare in nobleness with the purple violet," once wrote a mediaeval bishop to his friend, an abbess queen. In a fifteenth-century manuscript violets are listed among "herbes for potage" and also among "herbes for sauce"; "vyolette flourez" are "for a salade." The Goodman of Paris put violet leaves in his herb omelette; fifteenth-century cooks made violet fritters and a kind of custard

called "mon ami" which was garnished with violets. For fevers, *Banckes's Herbal* recommends that one "heat oil of violet meddled with powder of poppy seed and anoint the small of the back therewith....Also, for him that may not sleep for sickness, seethe this herb in water and at even let him soak well his feet in the water...and when he goeth to bed, bind this herb to his temples." Violets were also good for sore eyes, falling fits, and drunkenness. The Goodman of Paris brought his violets indoors before frost. ⌡ Candied violets are still considered a delicacy by certain people, and violet leaves a welcome addition to salads. Tincture of violets made from the whole fresh plant is considered useful for a spasmodic cough, and poultices of the fresh leaves will help to allay pain. Since the making of perfume from violets is an expensive process, most violet perfumes on the market today are made from other sources.

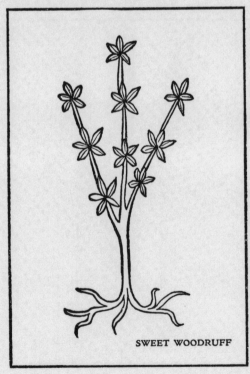

SWEET WOODRUFF

Woodruff, Sweet   **Asperula odorata, L.**

Sweet woodruff, when dried, has a scent like new-mown hay. It was used for strewing on floors, perfuming clothes in chests, and making garlands for churches on feast days. "It is good for healing all sicknesses that come from heat," states the *Hortus sanitatis*, and "the drops of dew lie a long time on this herb." ❡ The dried herb is still used to perfume linens and is said to keep away moths. In Germany sprigs of woodruff are steeped in Rhine wine to make a delicious drink called *Maibowle*.

Index of Herbs by Common Names

Index of Herbs by Botanical Names

THE BOOK WAS DESIGNED BY FRANZ C. HESS.
THE HEADINGS ARE SET IN GOUDY TEXT;
THE TEXT IS SET IN 12 POINT CLOISTER OLD STYLE.
THIS SEVENTH PRINTING WAS DONE
BY THE EILERT PRINTING COMPANY.

From Le Fournier's DECORATION D'HUMAINE NATURE ET ADORNEMENT DES DAMES,
Paris, Pierre Leber, 1533